IF YOU WERE A KID DOCKING AT THE
International Space Station

BY JOSH GREGORY • ILLUSTRATED BY JASON RAISH

CHILDREN'S PRESS® An Imprint of Scholastic Inc.

Content Consultant
Margo Godon, Program Manager, Kymeta Government Solutions, Redmond, WA

NOTE TO THE READER, PARENT, LIBRARIAN, AND TEACHER: This book combines a historical fiction
narrative with nonfiction fact boxes. While all the nonfiction fact boxes are historically accurate
and true, the fiction comes solely from the imaginations of the author and illustrator.

Photos ©: 9 top: robert_s/Shutterstock; 9 bottom: 3Dsculptor/Shutterstock; 13: Bill Ingalls/NASA; 15: Science
Source; 17 top: JSC/NASA; 17 bottom: NASA/age fotostock; 19: NASA Photo/Alamy Images; 21: JSC/
NASA; 23: MSFC/NASA; 25: Andrey Armyagov/Alamy Images; 27: Karen Nyberg/NASA.

Library of Congress Cataloging-in-Publication Data
Names: Gregory, Josh, author. | Raish, Jason, illustrator.
Title: If you were a kid docking at the International Space Station / by Josh Gregory ; illustrated by Jason Raish.
Other titles: If you were a kid.
Description: New York, NY : Children's Press, an imprint of Scholastic Inc., [2018] |
Series: If you were a kid | Includes bibliographical references and index.
Identifiers: LCCN 2017005111 | ISBN 9780531237465 (library binding : alk.paper) | ISBN 9780531239476 (pbk. : alk. paper)
Subjects: LCSH: International Space Station—Juvenile literature. | Space stations—
Juvenile literature. | Outer space—Exploration—Juvenile literature.
Classification: LCC TL797.15 .G74 2018 | DDC 629.44/2—dc23
LC record available at https://lccn.loc.gov/2017005111

All rights reserved. Published in 2018 by Children's Press, an imprint of Scholastic Inc.
Printed in the United States of America 113

SCHOLASTIC, CHILDREN'S PRESS, and associated logos are trademarks and/or registered trademarks of
Scholastic Inc., 557 Broadway, New York, NY 10012.

1 2 3 4 5 6 7 8 9 10 R 27 26 25 24 23 22 21 20 19 18

TABLE OF CONTENTS

357 feet (109 m)

240 feet (73 m)

Looking Into Space

In 1961, Russian **cosmonaut** Yuri Gagarin became the first human to travel into outer space. Since then, many more explorers have blasted off toward the stars. Their missions have taught us a lot about our **solar system** and the rest of the universe, but there is still more to learn.

One way astronauts study outer space is by visiting space stations to perform research. The first space station was built in the early 1970s. Space stations are huge spacecraft where astronauts can live and work in space for months at a time. Today, most astronauts around the world share a single space station called the International Space Station, or ISS.

Turn the page to go on an incredible space station adventure. You will see that traveling to outer space can offer you a new view of our world.

Meet Lucy!

Lucy Robinson dreams of becoming an astronaut one day, just like her older cousin Marie. She knows it won't be easy. But she tries to learn everything she can about science and space travel. Every time Marie visits, Lucy has a long list of questions to ask about her job . . .

Meet Tim!

Tim is Lucy's younger brother. Like his sister, he looks up to their cousin Marie. He would love to be a part of a mission to outer space. There's only one problem: He is afraid of heights! Every time he sees a video of a rocket blasting off, he wonders how astronauts can be so brave . . .

The whole family had gathered at Lucy and Tim's house to wish Marie good luck. In just a few days, she would be taking her first trip into outer space. Lucy was thrilled for her cousin. What an amazing adventure! Tim was excited, too. But he was also a little scared. Would Marie be safe up in space?

THE PULL OF GRAVITY

Gravity is a force that pulls objects toward each other. Large objects such as planets have a lot of gravity. This is what keeps you stuck to Earth's surface. Earth's gravity also keeps the ISS in **orbit** around the planet. But the farther apart objects are, the weaker gravity between them is. This is why Earth's gravity is not strong enough to pull the ISS all the way to the ground.

"Marie, what kind of training did you have to do before the mission?" asked Lucy.

Marie explained that she and the other astronauts had practiced space travel in **simulators**. They also took classes to learn about the technology they would be using aboard the space station. Marie had to learn to speak Russian, too. This way she could talk to the cosmonauts who were joining her on the mission.

10

FAR FROM HOME

The ISS is always about 250 miles (402 kilometers) from Earth's surface. That might seem like a long way. But compared to other things in space, it's not that far at all. The moon is almost 239,000 miles (384,633 km) from Earth. The sun is almost 93 million miles (149.7 million km) away!

Distance from moon to Earth: 239,000 miles (384,633 km)

Distance from ISS to Earth: 250 miles (402 km)

Illustration not to scale

"How will you get to the space station?" Tim asked. "Will you be safe?"

Marie chuckled. She explained that she would first travel to Kazakhstan. From there, she would board a small spacecraft that would launch into space and **dock** with the space station. She promised Tim that many other astronauts had made the trip safely before.

KAZAKHSTAN

TO SPACE AND BACK

All trips to the ISS begin and end in Kazakhstan. Three astronauts at a time climb aboard a Russian Soyuz spacecraft. After blasting off, it takes them about six hours to reach the ISS. When it is time to return to Earth, usually after about six months, the astronauts get back in the same Soyuz spacecraft. On the return trip, it takes about three and a half hours to land back in Kazakhstan.

A Soyuz spacecraft blasts off toward the ISS.

It was getting late. Everyone hugged Marie and wished her luck as she got ready to leave. Tim handed her Rex, his favorite stuffed dog. "Please take Rex with you," he said. "He'll keep you safe!"

Marie thanked him and promised to bring Rex into space. She also promised to stay in touch from the space station with video chat. Lucy and Tim exchanged an excited glance. They couldn't believe such a thing was possible!

SPACE STUDIES

Astronauts spend much of their time aboard the ISS performing science experiments and collecting information. Sometimes they run tests on themselves to see how human bodies react to being in outer space. They have studied ways of growing food in space. They've observed the movement of big storms on Earth. And they have tested the ways that different machines react to being left outside in space.

A Russian cosmonaut collects lettuce leaves grown aboard the ISS as part of an experiment.

That weekend, Lucy and Tim asked their mom to take them to the library. They wanted to learn more about space travel and the ISS. At a computer, Lucy was wowed by a video showing how the ISS was built. Meanwhile, Tim read a book that talked about space travel disasters. It made him more worried than ever.

BUILDING THE ISS

The ISS is made of many smaller pieces called **modules**. Each module is built on Earth and then launched into space. Astronauts connect the modules together. The first piece of the ISS was launched into orbit in 1998. Since then, many new modules have been added. They provide more room for astronauts, more tools for conducting experiments, and other benefits. The ISS is currently about the size of a six-bedroom house on the inside, and it is still growing. More new modules are planned for the future.

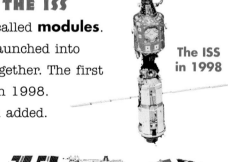

The ISS in 1998

The ISS in 2011

17

Disasters in Space

"Wouldn't it be great to go into space like Marie?" Lucy asked. "Just think of the amazing things she will get to see!"

"I don't know," Tim answered. "Space is really cool, but what happens if something goes wrong?"

"It does seem like it could be scary," Lucy admitted. "But that's what makes astronauts so awesome. They're smart and brave!"

Tim sighed. He wished he was brave like Marie and Lucy.

18

FLOATING IN SPACE

Aboard the ISS, astronauts do not walk around like we do on Earth. Instead, they float through the air. This is because of the way gravity works aboard the space station. Everything aboard the ISS stays in midair all the time unless it is strapped down.

An astronaut takes photos while floating aboard the ISS.

SOYUZ STAGE 3

AGE 2

A few weeks later, Lucy and Tim got the chance to have a video chat with Marie. Even though she was up in space, they could see her talking right there on their tablet.

"Wow!" said Lucy. "I feel like I'm on the space station with you!"

Marie held Rex up to the camera to show Tim. "Everything went perfectly, and we're safe and sound aboard the ISS," she said. She told them about life on the space station. She even showed off some of the special food the astronauts ate. It was dried out so it would last a long time without spoiling.

A SAFE PLACE IN SPACE

Humans are not naturally suited to survive in outer space. It is very cold, there is no oxygen to breathe, and the air pressure is deadly. To live aboard the ISS, astronauts rely on a variety of life-support technology. Machines create breathable air and control the temperature and air pressure. Astronauts must keep careful watch over these systems. If something were to go wrong, their lives would be in danger.

A NASA astronaut works on the ISS's water recycling system.

21

Marie told her cousins about a day she had to repair something on the outside of the space station. She had to put on a space suit and do a space walk to help fix the problem.

"It was one of the most amazing things I've ever done," said Marie. "I could see Earth floating way down beneath my feet, with nothing in between. It was beautiful!"

Lucy and Tim were almost too amazed to respond.

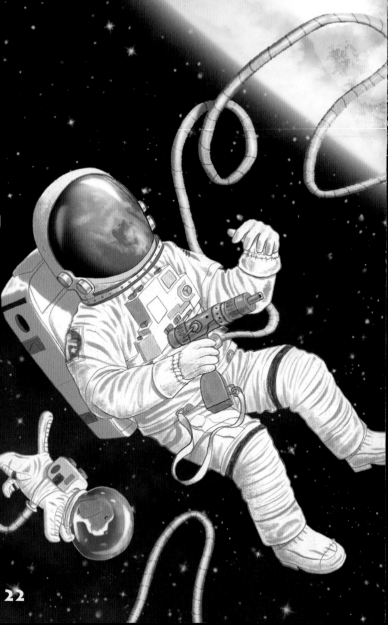

MAKING REPAIRS

Just like any machine or technology, the ISS needs maintenance to stay in working condition. If something on the outside of the spacecraft needs work, astronauts might put on space suits and go fix it. While spacewalking, they must always stay connected to the space station with a **tether**. This keeps them from floating away.

A NASA astronaut works to install new equipment on the outside of the ISS.

Tether

About six months after she had left, Marie was finally back home on Earth. To celebrate, the whole family gathered once again at Lucy and Tim's house. As usual, the kids had plenty of questions for her. But first, Marie had to return Rex to Tim.

"Thanks for letting him come with me," she said. "He helped keep me from getting lonely up there."

"Wow," said Tim. "I can't believe Rex went all the way to space."

"Maybe one day, you and I can follow in his footsteps," Lucy said with a grin.

SPEEDING THROUGH SPACE

The ISS is constantly in motion as it orbits Earth. It moves at a speed of about 17,200 miles per hour (27,681 kph). It travels all the way around the world more than 15 times per day. This means the people aboard see the sunrise about every 90 minutes!

An astronaut works in space as the sun rises over Earth.

"I don't know," Tim replied. "I'm still not sure I want to go all the way to space."

"That's okay," said Marie. "We need plenty of people back on Earth to work in mission control."

"Yeah!" said Lucy. "I'll be an astronaut, and you can run the missions."

Tim smiled and said, "That sounds like a great plan to me!"

ENERGY FROM THE SUN

The ISS is packed with computers, machines, and other things that need electricity to work. So where does this energy come from? The sun! The ISS is equipped with enough solar panels to cover about half of a football field. The panels absorb sunlight and turn it into electricity. When the space station is in Earth's shadow, it relies on batteries for power.

Solar panels on the ISS

Our Solar System

NEPTUNE

URANUS

SATURN

JUPITER

MARS

VENUS

MERCURY

MOON

ISS

EARTH

Note: Map is not to scale

28

Timeline

1957 Russia launches *Sputnik*, the world's first satellite.

1961 Yuri Gagarin becomes the first human to travel into space.

1969 Neil Armstrong and Buzz Aldrin become the first humans to set foot on the moon.

1971 Russia launches *Salyut 1*, the first space station.

1998 The first module of the ISS is launched into orbit.

2000– present The ISS is continually occupied by three to six crew members at a time, with groups of three leaving and returning every six months or so.

Words to Know

cosmonaut (KAHZ-muh-nawt) the Russian term for an astronaut

dock (DAHK) to connect one spacecraft to another

modules (MAH-joolz) smaller pieces that can be arranged in different ways to form a larger object

orbit (OR-bit) the curved path followed by a satellite, space station, or other object as it circles a star or planet

simulators (SIM-yuh-lay-turz) machines that allow people to experience something or practice performing a task by imitating real-life conditions

solar system (SOH-lur SIS-tuhm) a star and all the planets and other objects that orbit it

tether (TEH-thur) a ropelike device used to keep two things connected

Index

ABOUT THE AUTHOR

Josh Gregory is the author of more than 90 books for kids. He has written about everything from animals to technology to history. A graduate of the University of Missouri–Columbia, he currently lives in Portland, Oregon.

ABOUT THE ILLUSTRATOR

Jason Raish is an illustrator living in Brooklyn, New York. He has also lived in Seoul, Beijing, Tokyo, Barcelona, London, and Paris, because new experiences make him a better artist. He wishes he could experience outer space.

Visit this Scholastic website for more information about the International Space Station: www.factsfornow.scholastic.com Enter the keywords **International Space Station**